www.finishinglinepress.com

The Drowning Book

poems by

Cristina J. Baptista

Finishing Line Press
Georgetown, Kentucky

The Drowning Book

ACKNOWLEDGMENTS

"Trouble Woman" first appeared in *Structo Magazine* (Issue 14, August 2015)

"Eleven" first appeared in *Right Hand Pointing* (Issue 91, October 2015)

Thank you to *Structo* and *Right Hand Pointing*, who first published some of the
poems in this collection; and to Finishing Line Press for helping me see the value
in my own work, as well as for supporting my vision.

To Li Yun Alvarado, Todd Colby, Elisabeth Frost, Caroline Hagood, and Jordan
Windholz: I cannot thank you enough for your selfless support, enthusiasm,
energy, poetic discussions, and inspiration.

To my students, whose words spark in me the most surprising, unexpected fuel
to get the fire roaring: you are among these poems more than you know.

Finally, thank you to my family and friends—who don't always understand but
continue to support me with words of encouragement and faith.

Publisher: Leah Maines
Editor: Christen Kincaid
Cover Art: Daniel Berry Austin (Photographer)
Author Photo: Cristina J. Baptista
Cover Design: Elizabeth Maines McCleavy

Printed in the USA on acid-free paper.
Order online: www.finishinglinepress.com
also available on amazon.com

Author inquiries and mail orders:
Finishing Line Press
P. O. Box 1626
Georgetown, Kentucky 40324
U. S. A.

Table of Contents

"All I can say is that things will happen. Just what, I don't know."

Carson McCullers

Trouble Woman

after psalm 6

To be hoarse in the throat is my fault and forgiveness,
       a pensive stare of sound; a tremble of teeth, not fingers,
       and the gaping wound of mouth that cannot press or moan.

I ought to be lashed to rocks due to my mother's boastfulness,
       slung over shoulders, secured as a slouching shadow
       for fear I could slay my fathers (for I have had many).

I have blundered my way into life like the banshee
       whose knees were always chafed from apple tree climbs
       and bones always ached from overreaching.

What an unladylike thing to do—wearing shorts, and sleeveless.
       I may as well be naked like shoal, use myself to fill up cracks,
       pressing fingers against wounds, as if to stop

them up, but only tearing, warping wrapped hands—this clay
       around a candle, itself a cupping, a bursting
       in a stigmata of flame. How the heat hardens!

For I have been *that* desperate and shamed, one blow away
       from snuffing out enemies. Sometimes, I am slinking stoat;
       often, I am hooded crow, my throat dark as ink and enigma.

And I have filled my eyes with mirrors, accumulated
       a life built from scraps of looking
       at the concave backs of spoons, faces

in car windows, passing, wide as the breadth of a liquid
       pool. Everything is a surface preparing
       to break, a first time. A last time—a surface, filling.

Now, no urgency feels more reckless than this, prompting
       me to swallow thoughts, abandon sense
       of precaution that always chases

my bones, now useless. Overnight, repression
          sprung in boisterous guilty gait, one catastrophe
          after another, even my body a foreign thing

in need of trimming. Had I known
          it would be so easy to lose myself in mourning,
          I would have done it years ago.

Daguerreotype of Water & Bone

with a line from Kate Chopin

Rain falling like Thelonious Monk composed it,
only summer heat reveals the way her face looked as a child—curl and frizz
around edge, portrait out of focus or coming in.
Hair growing in bursts like hyacinths.

In those fuzzy parts is the dust of conjuring fingertips,
the way my mother reached her smaller hand to touch my wrist, click
at the protrusion, as if all of me was a mistake, those bones rooted deep.
In the rain is mercury vapor, to give rise to my longing

to have back the thinness that incites tongue clicks, excites
concern. To be noticed beyond a vanishing mist—worthy
of tracings, invisible scrimshaw, an awareness of how I grow
or shrink, how I move as a human being testing the light.

Some tarnish is a natural thing, especially where the fingers have held,
the way a child fixes her hand in a mother's, if only with her eyes.
These are the shocking things: metal delicate as skin
with veins blue as skim milk ringing a bottle's lip.

I can tell you that the nights are no holier than the days, but she did not
     come back
and nothing was left but shadow, as she walked into the sun
and dreamt of stars; as her impatience grew with the waiting.
Even photographs endure the indignity of fumes

and although everything I say feels so small,
I could crack open the rain
with a snap of my fingers, the bones so familiar
in the swift flow of blood between.

Tell me more about the woman who did not come back.
No one to answer, as if, perhaps, I am that woman, still
in the process of some unintelligible movement,

an unhinging, small as the shifting of sand or the rotation of the earth

and I cannot understand if I am coming or going.
However you slice a fruit, there is only one way
to eat it: with the mouth. Again, reminded of limitations
and how hard we work to go beyond them.

How often it feels as if every person
must make her attempt to stop the world, to pause and, when no
    one's looking,
readjust all the joints; how all water is a mirage of blue,
how all blue, an answer for thirst.

Remnants

"Bury your bodies deep," my mother said,
"but your bones deeper."

She wanted me to slip away to the moment just before
disappearance meant that she, herself, could not be "mother."

It is in the letting go that the greatest beauty can be spared
for another generation, its coat of rust an armor, natural as limestone

and the way everyone forgets that it is not "stone" at all,
but remains. Don't pillage from the dead, or walk in their shoes. Live in their
   skulls,

every portal filling into a home where futures perish
like drifting cities. "No," mother says; "these are not yours to hold,

these reflections on the water. But keep your back straight, and hands cupped
   just so,
and you can fill them with the weight of anything worth holding."

Who are we but the metacarpals and spleens of others
on some strange revolving contraption that carries

and kills? Sometime in the future, our belly buttons
will be galaxies of accumulated dust, for ash and rubble

are two things upon which we can depend
to raise our cities of more bodies, to build more boats

and salute more ships before we sink
them. Funny—how everything made for water has to start

with a little clay, a little earthiness riding up the nostrils.
Funny how death by drowning is still a falling to rock-bottom,

the spirit releasing itself just a little faster
in the untethered rise to surface,

unless trapped in some monstrous belly, an iron mouth,
or ghastly gash of torn intestines gushing water into more water

where the only eyes that can see blink the unreadable code
left for plankton and some mighty God, a withdrawing hook beyond reach.

As a wanderer of the sea, you learn several immediate truths,
all of them ways to die;

to look no one in the eye, to get out of the way,
to let the body drive and rock and wedge.

When insufficiently wet, rope pulled too quick can burn
like the time a spark caught a ride on a tumbleweed in Alcanena

and dazzled the mountainside with a red fury for weeks, rock
and grain dark as a sunburned sailor, and the townspeople

let even the smallest children scout for those who may have been overlooked,
because there was no one else to count the bodies.

Saving the Girl

Although Ma never allowed the daughter to use real knives
until she was in the double-digits, this trial

never stopped her from taking risks and doing
anything she believed in. Even when she believed in lies, she balanced

on edges with the readiness of fledglings, not knowing better.
Bruises, cuts, and slivers were welcome to live in this body

as sanctuary. She worshipped ragged red flows, the way burs clung to her
hairy legs, the same legs kids at school called "gorilla limbs"

and asked her why she didn't get a razor? Instead, she pounded a fist
once through a glass window, trying to shake off bees.

While her Papa stood with her at the bathroom sink, holding her grip
under running water, she watched his reflection in the mirror, ignored him

and his words of "what will your mother say?" The water felt like nothing.
He drew a smiley-face in red mecuricome and all she thought of

was shattered glass held in the frame, tearing
in the pattern of eggshells, where the membrane cleaves

even in the cleaving. It is nature to clutch. Everything,
even shards. It is nature to believe in opposites,

one parent locking up the knives, the other,
insisting, "be strong." They had to break her open

to mend better, to re-forge. Her caution grew, but, of course she stayed a
    rebel—
she had curly hair from Papa, after all.

Everything that breaks knits slow, tedious. The threading of a needle. An
    interweaving,
to hold a button in place, the way a stuffed animal's eye

can be stitched back into place, and the mending will allow it to continue
not seeing and pretending to see. While a fracture point may yield to pressure,

then again,
it may not yield at all. It may be pretense

holding the whole thing together. Simulacrum—a drawing brushed
over a deep wound that needed stitches. If only Papa hadn't had to go to work.

In the kitchen: the mother counts the cutlery, folds it away in cloth
napkins at the back of the drawer.

In the garage: the father cups her hands like spoons,
pours in BB-gun pellets too small to tell if they're warm or cool.

Anything can happen with such secrets sweeping about the same house
but, here is the truth: nothing did. Not to her.

Meanwhile, the parents cracked imperceptibly. Later—slices letting out
the bad blood, then—sliding in pieces. Slipping away. An overseas breakage.

Protection is a selfish act

yet it breeds strong people who feel, who know,
who fear a life without having tried.

Eleven

As Adam slept, his rib was taken,
the dozen pairs shaken,
perhaps left with one less thoracic vertebra,

like sections of an orange freed
from their binding—a book loosed of pages.
Sometimes, an orange is called "apple from China,"
this speculation a reminder of that first Garden.

In Portugal, my grandfather grafted oranges to other trees,
all flesh a playground for creation,
his hands as nimble as any other's.

God closed up the hole in Adam's side,
it is written, like punching
a fist through water and watching
the space refill when the hand is withdrawn.

When Light Strikes the Body

it is a great wrangler,
showing no mercy.

It bent nature against itself,
hooked and dangerous, turned Niagara Falls into a power station,
harnessing.

It must have been a shock, seeing
that first body beneath that first light bulb,
all imagined imperfections proven,
spirits rising from the dead.

Smudging its way through, a map arises,
cities and roads, cupping wounds like potholes
where fingers could push,
wondering how many others had been there first.

"Light" can mean the lack of weight, each breast
a broken pendulum, a crooked scale dragged down
on one side, buoying up the other.

Let me get this off my chest
(without exposing every ridge of a sternum,
every gap of myself, every outward thrust):
it's not my business what you do with your body
and it isn't your business what I do with mine.

Regardless,
I love my body enough to keep it for me,
bathed in light
fabrics.

How heated must a body be before it's called
incandescent, how slick beneath a lone bulb?
How blistered by noon,
sprawled behind a garden wall?

How we fill the air with transmissions bouncing
off our sleek skins.

In the Louvre, Drost's Bathsheba finds the light slanting
head to breast, a rippling tear,
hands hidden in shadow.
Light just another draping, an impasto
tempting fingers and devouring eyes.

Rembrandt's Bathsheba has plowman's hands,
overshadowing her other parts,
a distraction fooling no one,
hands that could wrestle open warped drawers,
unscrew pickle jar lids, tug a chifforobe into place.

I can't believe that God strung sunlight
between tree branches
because humans can't be trusted
to hold something so precious, even with two hands,

how a nipple is an impossible eruption,
uncoerced, a disruption of the body's plane,
a stigmata as much as a flame from a candle
following a path of air like an eye trained
only to see what isn't there.

"Is nothing sacred?" my mother asks,
and I have nothing to say,
although I shake my head where she cannot see,
seventy-five miles away, the other end of invisible wires

that still manage to pull like threads.
"Are these the heartstrings?" I want to ask,
"tugging from my exposed breast?"

I want to tell her, "We tried to be sacred once,
but became scared instead."

But she is gone, hung up
(a term we still use though there's nothing to hang,
only a slackness and a letting go),
her sleeves rustling in some room
so familiar, she never notices the mirror anymore,

the way it takes a single bulb
and makes the ugly stark thing tucked behind a lampshade
into a chandelier, the body decked and dimpled,
begging to be read—a book and its deckled edges.

Hawthorn

for Ferguson, MO—the Missouri state flower and symbol is the hawthorn.

In all growing, something must break,
as the hawthorn seed requires stratification—
a pretreating, a stimulation of winter.
Only then is it forced from dormancy,

a whole other beast.
Everything is an illusion—give it time
and it will shift and shape, turn again
and again and against you.

Celtic lore says the hawthorn can heal a broken heart.
In Gaelic, it marks the entrance to the Otherworld.
We are caught somewhere between
this and that, the fruit and thorn.

And fruit has led us down so many wrong
paths before; have we learned so little?
The first loss was for the sake of a single bite,
yet, rapacious, teeth do not stop

as if biting is the only object of a mouth

when words will do.
We have to stretch love, and feed it.
Communicate it. Splice it on what lives,
not sink it into stale dust.

Even 7000 years before Lazarus, hawthorns aroused
the near-dead: traces of berries found in pottery jugs
contained beverages, archeologists say,
religious and medical—the same thing. Spirit and body.

The same thing. Moses' Burning Bush;
Christ's crucifixion crown—all hawthorns,
or rumored to be. Is or may be—eventually,
the same thing.

While events change in time
because the mind is nimble and mutable,
suspicious, in hindsight, even to the self,
feeling is not so fleeting. It is why symbols

persist, myths endure, even when the real stories
are buried, one shovel of earth at a time.
But this is the only way to plant
something new and remarkable.

When it flowers in Spring, the hawthorn is showy,
white,
encouraged in the promise of fruits
by August or September—red,

which fall quickly.

"Flowering thorn," they call the hawthorn,
related to the rose. When Fall comes,
green and yellowed leaves ripen
to burgundy, expose more thorns,

the barren smoothness of its bark visible.
The truth is, a world of fear is just a world—
and there's little to do about it. Leaves will always fall
and we must only watch, and take out the rake

or let things be. There is no putting-back, no mending
of the fading plant. There is only what is left
behind, thriving life beneath wood.
Put your ear to the heart and listen.

That is truth—not kindling piled for burning.

The hawthorn is target to infiltrators—
voracious moths, leaf rusts, and fire-
blight. But it fights back with its thorns,
which it cannot help. This is its heritage,

remember. The rose. The fruit. The blight.

In stratification, seeds grow
from cold, moist soil. With what do we wet
such a land as this—asphalt, not earth?
Shrill coldness of fear? The stain of blood?

(How much, in the right light,
each tree is a shrouded figure,
bent and ductile, as if carrying,
across splayed shadows, its own cross.)

Now, the hawthorn stretches its branches,
curved like misplaced parentheses,
baskets or arms flung, a desperate mother,
where all crash down.

As the hawthorn stands and signals life,
it studs itself with thorns not of spite, but nature,
remember. It tears the manmade spaces
wide open. How often do we find roots

creeping from fissures in foundations,
sprouting slips from sidewalk cracks?
A tile loosened by an errant sapling,
a brick chewed by eager moss?

Ancient Greeks and Romans worshipped the hawthorn
for luck. Welsh fishermen carry its thorns,
fondle them in pockets while praying for good catches.
With imagination, we make the best of dangers. We endure.

In all breaking, something must grow.

Things Unseen

with an excerpt from Langston Hughes

1.
They say that women are flowers,
crumpled, I suppose,
especially at the end of evenings when anything can happen
and does.

Some float like water lilies, even look the work
of Monet—women with faces
better viewed from a distance, and beneath
the gauze of alcohol.

Let me tell you this: we are not the things
we imagine. Memory is little more
than petals to conceal the central hold
we have on ourselves.

I cannot despise people for trying
to force my memory more than they force
my hands, more than they force
me. I leave myself to the trusting

and wander through elaborate gardens more than I recall,
never stopping to look at flowers
for—I confess—I'm more often
reading cards, descriptions of baubles

with Latin names, words I feel good pronouncing
just right, even though—I confess again—
I haven't a clue. If a woman is supposed to look
like something else, is it possible

to *sound* like someone else? When I was in my 20s,
I'd visit the Botanical Gardens on Saturdays,
take my books, and wander. Several times,
visitors sent me shady looks,

as if I was serpentine in my limbs, sprawled
across the deciduous deliciousness.
To read beneath an arbor of broken
limbs feels the most true.

2.
I like that the year I was born, the USPS
released a stamp featuring a Motorcycle.
I was destined to always be going somewhere
on a historical machine, already too old to ride itself,
having uphill battles and to be hoisted—
Sisyphean and all that roar.

Nobody expects the hero of a novel
to be a *her*, on a motorcycle, although—
if she appears—people probably expect her
to be in impractical shoes
and too-tight-trousers,
black of course,

and snake-skin all over.
Now, what was that you were going to tell me about my youth?
That it was too short and too menacing to allow time
to learn to ride. I wanted to be like Nancy
Drew, who had licenses for everything—cars, boats, planes,
motorcycles. Who does that by 18?

Heroines in novels, that's who,
books for no shrinking violets, no wall-
flowers. Everybody has an opinion,
but in history, men have seemed to be the loudest
and, so, even above the roaring engines, the blast
of howitzers and screeching cannons,

they are remembered. In some homes,
howling babies will suffice as a proper substitute,

but let me tell you about that Drew girl:
she was everything and everyone
I wanted to be, from her titian hair to her 5'7" build,
and I thought I could fight everything,

even genetics. But that's not what this is all about.
This is about the act of getting away
and the girl who did it.

3.
Someday soon, they'll see how beautiful I am
and be ashamed that I am
the last to know
and see it. I've spent a lifetime avoiding mirrors
out of fear that I'll catch myself
the way Medusa did.
My mother used to call me that—because my hair
clogged the drain in snaky coils,
awakened in water, fattening

in some gorgeous creature
I was only half-ashamed to call my own.
My father was the one who said
I was getting vain, the way some people say,
turning their faces and pretending to fix a stack
of files that are already ordered,
you're getting fat.

In my bedroom, there were no mirrors,
and so I learned to look for answers everywhere
but the world I knew inside
that room. Books lined the walls where a vanity
may have stood,
and I turned towards the rubbed spines like erect
soldiers, played tunes invisibly among them
before I made a selection.

When the temperatures changed,
I was outside, and reading,
outside myself and ready. I found other mirrors,
like the bottom pane of the back-porch door,
which bloated my lower-half,

or the fragmented glass of the shed window,
where I'd punctured my fist
and broken the window by accident
while striking off bees. There, my head
floated, a sense of removal
from the spine.

Every life leads to this reflection:
that we are everywhere, even if we try to hide it.

Parents have the greatest ambitions, but nothing
matters so much as their own mirrored children,
the shrug of shoulders, the way in which they plant
apple trees in the backyard in hopes that grandkids
will someday find them desirable.

Even when the season was not long enough
to ripen half the foreign fruits in the garden,
my father planted them anyway, always hoping
for that something he'd tasted once
but never got to know again.

Sons of Daedalus *or* **How We Begin to Wonder**

How soon we forget that breathing
is not a learned thing, that all flying
is a cultivation of senses

our loftiest moments rising
on curled tongues
just as language is not created equally.

The palate curves to fit the speaker,
each nation lending to its bodies
the presence of a different roof of the mouth.

The soft British sounds even differ from
the English of America,
and its mouthing multitudes, pecking

like birds—hungry or desperate
or crying in despair. In all voices, all languages,
fear is heard the same.

The ear, curled in its labyrinth,
waits for a signal.
How long has everyone dreamt of flying

and kept the secret?
Fear of being found out
as different

comes with every age and age
comes to us faster and faster.
Many a good person has been called an imbecile;

if only we had listened sooner. Imagine
the first man who believed
in the possibility of flight

the possibility of being
more than rooted in earth
but suspended in the secret invisibility

of Babel,
without need for ladders or desperation
or split tongues.

Imagine *being* this first man who believed:
we can fly. Voicing
his opinions. Others must have

laughed and snorted, preposterous tones tripping
on sharp tongues, cleansed in acrid
wine and too-little wisdom.

The fear of flying is nothing
to the fear of not flying. Wings gathered
as hands, grasping at air—

pinions, which have two, almost opposite, meanings:
1.   the outer part of a bird's wing, including the flight feathers.
2.   to hold or pin someone down.

It's a shame that the good things
don't spread
as fast as fear.

So, so much for saying we are all the same inside.
Maybe—but not our mouths
and the way they say one thing

as we become another.
I was alone for so long
that the words snapped my tongue.

Speaking is a flight into battle,
a fight with air. Pushing
words forward, stacked like a phalanx.

I cannot even swallow the words
felled before I had a chance.
How often we forget ourselves

like heat, rising—
then—stopping. Returning to earth. How to clip
the wings. Power, in a reverse direction,

is still power,
each of us an heir to Icarus,
falling as we dream

dreaming as we fall.
When we stop living like we're gods,
we will then learn to fly.

The Young Physician

In the foreign city, behind a cathedral,
a child stitches the wall together with Band-Aids
stretched across the fissures,
tiny ladders thrusting in crooked curves,
their rungs peeling at white edges.
"Why'd you do it?" a stranger stops and asks, a net of apples
slung over a shoulder, as if he carries laundry, indifferent

to the bruising. The voice is a bird flung into glass.
The man needs no answer, but speaks to feel his tongue, having dreamt
the night before of the sounds of the horror—having felt, three miles away,
the tremble of the wall, heard its weeping like a brittle rib-crack.
"I wanted to save it," the girl whispers,
stepping off a wooden box pressed to the wall's base.
"I wanted to stop its bleeding."

Fourteen

Rings of a tree, sliced, revealing
dark and light, as if leaves
swallow not only morning but night sky,
leave stars alone for fingers
to read like Braille, or asterisks
with corresponding footnotes.

But I've misplaced the pages.

Maybe there was no apple tree, the Romans right
to call peaches "Persian apples." Here is a pit
to catch better in throats, to hew your breaths,
hold your heart high, caught in an unspeakable act.

I could read your scars only when carved,
the way a peach tree buries its wounds
much like the girl who planted it years ago.

Bravery

"Girl who braved 30-foot mid-Atlantic waves for hours dies"
Lisbon, Portugal, May 7, 2015

Everything I hear from my homeland
is a tragedy. The only way to make print
these days, is to die

so that the only people reading
about you
is anyone but.

There's a Stevie Smith poem about a woman
who is drowning, but on the shore,
her friends believe she's waving.

I wonder how long it took them
to decide to wave back,
if there was even a brief moment

of hesitance in their actions. I think that would help
me understand that people
are concerned for one another

and that we don't just go through the motions,
like when someone says "What's up?"
and you say, "good, and you?"

and then your voice drops
because you are a fraud
being, in those words,
found out.

This girl—the drowning girl
in the waters that brush the beaches
where I grew up walking

and climbing the *praia* walls—
must have been a brave child
to fight a quarter of her day

to survive. That is the human struggle
in all of us—the defiance of nature, despite
its indifference. We are made

of so much water and earth,
and always, the earth wins.
There is always a monster,

hers, thirty-feet and translucent
but she would never come to enjoy it,
the way light falls between shallow rocks and

skims the blue-green water at Praia de Nazaré,
the way people pretend to sink
but are really crouching

on the slabs of stone poised like temples,
squat and ancient,
at the base of the cliffs.

One year, my father and I walked the trail towards the old
lighthouse, the disappointing-looking one
that is nothing like postcards of New England,

as this shelter is long and wide, brown
as the wet sand, and broken at its temples.
We came to the shrine there, a sad

way off, and I had to wait patiently
to take a photograph, as I had limited
film, and an old woman in her blue dress

kept whirling around the scene,
watching to see if someone would
open the door. Inside,

a smuggled statue left from the Moor
invasion. In the photograph: my father
standing, smiling, at the door, the woman's

back of the neck a blur in one corner, a swatch
of blue and black dress and sweater floating.
I wonder what this is,

this drowning out.

Two & Seven

Two

Tel Tzora tombs, father, and son
whose hands tore lions in tissue-like halves.
Twice, God's messenger promised
a strong son— *but—he must never cut his hair.*
Once, tied with two ropes, Samson erupted, slayed
Philistines with an ass' jawbone wielded like a bow,
bodies arrows clearing the moon.
Then, eyes gouged, forced grinding grain,
turning a millstone, ushering sky's collapse.
Later, begged *return my strength, just this once.*
Clutching pillars in Dagon, two hands forced crisis
until crushed. Some say Samson tore mountains
from secret roots, raised two overhead and struck,
making fire.

Seven

What if the Seals are bound not by wax
but with the seven locks of Samson's hair?
I've seen books with covers of human skin, words more tattoos
or totems than language, scrimshawed stories
more heard than told, covers pressed lips
sighing. How often words
are lies—even The Bible
speaks of seven angels setting seven bowls.
You must understand the euphemism:
"bowls" are plagues, nothing to fill
like a demanding vessel,
like a wooden cup scraped clean,
like a cleansed bone cut from flesh,
the body a forest cleared.

Sink the Line

No one in my family has ever learned to swim
although we are from a peninsula
and live in New England,
have always kissed our Atlantic
      (from both sides)
as if this, itself, would keep

it at bay

and far from our lungs.
Is this our hopefulness or foolishness,
despite that we are a watery people,
a lineage of seamen and whalemen,
fishermen and navy men

who have forgotten how to unhook,
      how to disengage,
           that cleaving is itself an illusion,
      the very opposite
of all promises. We have neglected

the line
and made ourselves into walkers
who have little time for oceans,
and in our sparing,
have little time for people

and in our sparring
have erased materials
(of a family).

Now, I look at photo
albums and find no names
transcribed on the backs of pictures,
and those few in which
I do recognize the subjects are mislabled:
for how could this photograph of my father

as a small child with hair golden
even in black-and-white, be from "1974,"
as is written on the flaky underside

in flagrant European script, with its draping
and cross-stitched numbers, "7"
looking like a hangman's prop.
More likely, it is the mid-1950s

      (but not
      even 1954, not even the "7" a mistake

      for the "5"),

and I wonder if my Papa
knew that, one day, he'd be back here, at this spot,
cresting in the rising wave, the push

of time, back
with his older brother, sleeping
and not standing, at this address, the house
once his grandmother's.

How many times do we spot mistakes,
saying, "I'll fix that later," but before
we know it, we are left to wait
for the "later" and the "fix" of something better?
When left too long in albums,

photographs will fuse to the cardboard,
the adhesive a molten glue, the contents
of past and present melting into inestimable
greatness of a mess. This is not symbolic—
it can't be,

even if there is the mimicry of an ocean,
the surging of a silent, crystalline wave below

the surface of the photograph, bulging its edges,
sagging the bodies.

There are only four women
in this line left
to preserve our roots here,
four women, all childless, all 30 or older.
Our time is a drying-up,
the harvesting of hay-like hair

and the withering. Is it our fault,
always turning from the water,
always failing to fuel ourselves,
yet always giving way to drowning
because we never learned to swim?

Tracking Faces

She kept her face in her bag,
getting on the train
one woman, emerging
five stops and one state later,
another—a stranger

shifting the scent of her arms,
shade of her face shaped
with the aroused touches of an
acrobat-cum-illusionist,
streamlining cheekbones—

only to evaporate in the sea of lanky girls
watching legs grow leaner
as they pass windowed shops,
like pros, knowing where to find the most flattering reflections
to taper a calf, trim a thigh.

Putting out an arm, I catch the way birthmarks follow me
in threes, tempting me to connect these places.
To what map does this skin lead
if not to an inner landscape where wilts
momentum and soul? A sluggish pulling into the station.

How it is possible to not recognize
even one's own hands,
traced on paper,
lines thicker than skin
and half crooked like truth.

First there was the child, then the creature
unhooking its jaw
and leaving it on the trail-side—
shucked skin spent on the sleepers. This is the way to birth
a woman. This is the way to ensure silence:

the lessening of movement, the forced inquiry
of eyes only,
the limping injury of time and material.
After enough track has passed,
it doesn't seem so strange

to hold the book wrapped
in human skin, to uncork its scent and breathe
in luxurious deepness on the train where
you'll never see anyone again,
at least, not with those faces.

Ornithology Book

Some boys will pull the feathers off birds
that are still alive, because they (the boys) are brave
or cowardly. My brother pulled the pages
out of books, and crushed their spines,
poor crippled creatures;
then scribbled on the loose flyleaves as if casts
on arms or legs, or slings on wings,
but never were they messages of encouragement or get well.

One year, during summer or pre-fall, before school had begun
(perhaps I was too young to be in school)
and while Papa snored inside on the couch,
my brother crept across the slick cover
on clover and milkweed
and trapped a small grey bird, pinned
beneath a yellow sand-bucket. His glee
lit the world in fiendish licks of green and fancy.

I looked on, took hold of the moment,
half-debating if this was madness or euphoria, did not know
a thing about repercussions. The word itself
was too long. The lip
of the bucket pressed against the bird's beak,
and there was a sound like the snap of the thinnest twig,
soft and sparing,
suffocating the fellow instantly.

> This memory drifts like the subtle-slow
> fall of down that loosens out the seams of a black
> winter coat. I keep picking feathers out
> of my hair and off the back
> of my driver's seat, but never absentmindedly. I have them
> all fooled. I am far too aware now
> of causality. Because the reason I remember the dew and
> the grey bird pressed into silence against purple weeds
> cropped close like a nest, was because

it was me—me who held

the bucket down in a moment when my brother
deserted his daring and felt his fingers
thrill in another movement: he pretended to fly,
but buzzed like jet engines—did not whistle—
and glided from me. Even then,

he was breaking free,
getting away. I was left holding—no—
pressing—the world against everything I knew to be right.
My eyes never looked down.

I watched the shadows of my stocky older brother
leap over wet grass and slope across the twined trees,
three fused so close they look like one,
in the center of the backyard.

It is this growth, this growing dependency,
that keeps the world in motion.

I never said a thing—I let him take the blame.
That was complicity, and complacence.
He took it, too, like the bird took its death,
because he did not know it was me.
For all he knew, it *was* him, him the destroyer of
life, of song, the potential to get away. Him,
murderer of flight.

This was my escape: the lie. I have never doubted
my ability to be courageous; it's my ability
to be courageous despite repercussions I know all too well.
Now, I forgive myself and give homage to other transitory things
that fly like feathered hopefuls. I pluck from shelves
and read books, cradling their spines, turning
pages careful and slow, always cupping a hand
and using only two fingers each time,

as if to prevent the failure of life,
the gentle, nut-like cracking
of an old book's too-pulled-back cover,
of a stranger's innocent brown beak.

Reading the Mountain

To be uncertain in childhood
is every great blessing all at once.
Could we return to curiosity
and the need for questions,

we would be a better world,
wonder sustaining
more than bread; imagination
guiding, not just a gild.

In 1995, the road outside my great-
grandmother's house (always called
this, as if she were never married)
cupped the boundary-less

hook of mountainside, where wild land
sloped to the lower part of town,
where I spent my summer replaying
the art of falling in my head

and told no one. The house was squat,
Chimera digging in claws, as not to tumble.
We watchers behind flimsy curtains grimed
with decades' talcum crouched,

weary limbs poised, jungle
animals after too much feasting.
What was out there was anyone's guess,
just beyond that draping edge,

some sinister agenda of sky's end
with a name in some other language we hadn't bothered
to ask about, and the solstice
of light, the bedding

of rain sputtering cruelly in bursts
into ground too dry to take it in, so often burned
and rejecting, a fireworking vein
of refusing earth:

it was afraid. Mornings awoke
to goat bells, animals clacking
their way around the edge while kidding
in fiendish cackles, bucking and playing,

and I envied the fearlessness, the yawning
manner of their slow-opening mouths, the kicking
of perfect slim, strong haunches. They left
a trail of pellets, round and dark,

the ones my father—who has never been able
to taste or smell—was once tricked into eating
by his mischievous older brother,
such a thing an older brother would do,

I knew, finding myself in the same position.
We are alike, he and I—Papa and me—
these two inseparable beings at the time,
chasing the rims of dreams, the ends of things

in hopes of encountering the new beginning.
When I was a child, we slept beneath the window
of his childhood house, just across the street,
at the other side of the turn, out of sight,

spoiled by a window he never had as a child.
Sometimes, the loss of something is never felt
until another child asks a question
that makes the man aware of that splinter

extricating itself before drawing deeper.
He told me not to read, which would spoil
my mind; yet, he built me a bookcase
to tempt me to Portugal another summer,

back to the house where the land had broken
its claws once more, had shook its cloaked
back and retreated so that the front door
was moved to the side of the house.

This is our way of transforming faces,
the contradictions that "front" is now "side,"
that "don't read" means "but fill this case."
We are encouraged to live

a life on the sly, a life on the side,
as it slides and slopes and slips
and we learn to be okay, to kick high and tempt
anyway. Twenty years later, nothing

feels so snug as the imagined
falling, the sensation of thick book pages
rubbing my fingers, feeling so much
like the way rubble loosens from the desperate hand.

"Bomber Cries in Court"

after a newspaper headline

1.
This is how it all begins—the breaking
and the breaking down. Funny

how all parts of us are fusion,
and the body's breaking makes

do with what it has to fix things.
Sometimes, we spring

a leak, as if this will curry favor
and help us sense ourselves

shrinking and shrieking beneath our skins.
How humbling is this tear

in all fabric, a reminder that life is granted
with no delusions that we all know what to do with it.

Nobody's perfect, but a perfect nobody can shatter the world.
It's the decent thing to do,

warn a daughter like this.
When I was a child, I could count

by the stars, marvel at them as if faces
after faces of people I would never meet.

There was a fissure in my mind then—
the cracks of iron that I could never hold

on my own, not with a body
as small as this.

2.

God tells us to "love one another like I have loved"
and you forget a word, and suddenly,

you don't find yourself anywhere. What voice
do those who don't believe in God hear?

What voice: that of another God, of another
place and the rising lump in the throat

that destroys all things? I imagine all memory
is a god that devours time,

in one hasty move, a long arm leaping
across the chessboard, saying nothing. He

leads us to the river in a sacrificial drowning,
in a pool made by indentations of remorse

and a blunt action. *Be strong:* my father's
only advice, two syllables, two blunt words.

Even that was enough. How I ache now to hear
them for the first time, as if appearing

more than some phantasmagoric presence,
the nerves in a finger, an unclipped thumbnail

outlined against the sun. If this is offense
or defense, I wish someone would tell me.

I could heave all strength
and still not know why.

3.
The apparition of these faces
is no Madonna or burning bush,

is an insurmountable problem.
To disengage from the effrontery

is to be less-human. How often we follow the guide-
lines of intention,

but people cannot follow in rows like ducks
or dominoes or people

shoving off into some holocaust.
The reality is that everyone is faceless

if no one is looking. Our intention
has never been clearer: encourage

looking, cultivate acceptance
that we are the sum of all parts

and our parts must stay whole,
or we become the misheard phrase,

the simple flaw that launches
all things backward.

4.
They tell us to love all things,
all people created equally. If only

life could be solved by hugging
anything within arms' reach.

When someone makes a headline,
I have to ask—*was he loved enough*

as a child? As a child
how could she do such a thing?

When do men and women stop being
boys and girls? When

do they cease being human beings?
That's what I want to know—where the pulsing

begins and ends,
as if it is a Transatlantic

wire that is constantly coming loose

and we still need to keep digging
and do the repairs.

Who wants to be a repairman nowadays?
Children are wanted for so much more than this,

to be bigger and better,
to be bombs.

Coming Back

"'Come on back in the shade,' he said. 'You mustn't feel that way.'"
Ernest Hemingway, "Hills Like White Elephants"

There's nothing so dark and lovely like moonlight,
and its cold bursts of anger on the ground,
a slab of concrete spare in its presence
that makes the perfect landing pad

for all lights from above.

Children are often warning,
shouting on the sidewalks,
"don't step on a crack!"
They never finish it—the way we did

when we were young. Now,
it's the same old story. Always the poor
mother, with her broken spine.
And where's the father? It's the question

I've always wondered and didn't ask.
What must be done
to break him? Is this a cruel thought? For children
to consider their massacres?

Even in school, we sang of Lizzie Borden
and her infamous axe, chanted
amongst dandelions and milkweed.
How brutal we all are to our parents,

our indifference to the reality of such agony
the worst offence. Even still,
no teacher ever intervened, shouted a "stop,"
explained our words

as meaning and pain and regret and sorrow—
reflection of ourselves. The shadings between us.
No teacher reminded us of anything
but to "play until the bell rings,"

half-hoping we'd grow tired and give her
or him peace of mind for the last half of the day
or year. It's clear to me, still: slouching
back to first-grade, sweetness tangled

in my hair, crumbs on my lips that my teacher
would brush with a gloved hand: "saving
a snack for later?" Now, you can't touch a child's
mouth and expect it will be wiped clean.

This is why we keep to corners and cut out light:
to retain the sense of ourselves that is, like sun,
hot and cold outside of the shadows. Now, I know
that there are some things

we cannot explain, like growing up,
growing into other people, and finding
that temptation is the best response
a remedy to doing nothing at all.

Tearing the Roots

Mother

> How can I tell you that my heart is a clattering
> like a swallowed key, a lost chord
>
> played against the windpipe, and all my words of aching
> cannot form the music meant to tell you
>
> how sharp is my love, how plowing. When my ribs
> crack, they are sounds of tinny hammers,
>
> bird-flapping beats against the body once
> part of yours.

Father

> As if missing you wasn't enough,
> how can I tell you I want to eat you shoes,
> just to taste where you've been
> without me,
> to figure out why you left,
> to learn the taste of leaving?

How to Master the Art of Motion

> "The best lack all conviction, while the worst
> Are full of passionate intensity."
> W. B. Yeats, "The Second Coming"

Step 1:
The ear presses itself
between ideas;
a mouth opens without pause
and utters irretrievable things, irredeemable—
a slouching voice, a demon-

stration extending from some body.
Spinning is a natural cure
for staying still. Even children know
how well they can offer a sense of progress
by leaping aboard the carousel.

How heavenly how all children are taught
by such well-informed adults
and their well-mannered ambitions lurking
against the rattling storm-door and screen-door
of a complacent mouth.

Lips secure in knowing no one expects words
to be action. Lips that are promises
and covers—confidential stamps
of people who speak big words, carry big sticks,
and choke them down.

Step 2:
"The only way to keep a secret
between two people
is to ensure one of them is dead,"
my mother always said.
Mothers always know.

If we keep the door open, we are Pandora
and her heirs, gathering doom in dark corners,
claiming it as our own.
Just because something is ours does not make it beautiful,
or right.

Now—such coyness in a thousand lips speaking Empty Words
in a thousand secret rooms of bright carpets—
lips pursing. Even children are told
to keep their secrets, as soon
as they are old enough to overhear.

Step 3:
Suture the mouth, tie the jaw.
Put coins on the eyes.
Mark the body with cairns.
There's no time like the present
to prepare for Lethe, and drink the water

of forgetfulness. Our mistake:
seeing what must be done
yet doing nothing. Even when we fail
and use the wrong words,
history makes no motion to correct us,

just as the story of Pandora, passed to children,
is a simple lie, a crease in a cloth,
unsmoothed; a mouth lined in parentheses of age.
It was not a Box at all, but a Jar; no corners,
but a curving form, a sweeping whorl for listening.

Cuts & Trims

"Get Eyebrows Like Brooke Shields!,"
wolfishly howled the headline
of an article I dared not read, recalling
my father's insistence that he liked Brooke Shields
without knowing anything about her.
"Her eyebrows aren't fussed
and she is natural." A knowing

nod, a scoff—as if keeping hands

off one's own body makes her
a greater good, a goddess.

In two languages, he could explain
how a wedding chamber is a magic act
behind-the-scenes event,
when the beauty removes her false
teeth, eyelashes, mole, hair.

My mother confessed that the reason she looked
so fashionable in her 1960s photos is that
she wore wigs, to preserve
the illusion of who she was. My father could
carve out "beauty" in two languages,
splitting syllables like seams. She starved—

an apple a day, sometimes,
a treat of a small popcorn, no butter.
Better that she did this. She whittled
and waited for love to happen,
which it did. Now, there's no sense
in her fixing her crooked grin
or the way she never shows teeth,
concealing the flaw that reminds her
of how human she is, despite all efforts.

She never smiles, this Portuguese Mona Lisa,
her lips a friction,
and mine—a doubt.

How can I be daughter to a fraud
and the exposer of such things? Who led them
onto this same path? It doesn't matter
what they yell at one another: anyone
who cannot hear could look
from a distance, and imagine them
conspiring. I believe in One God
and He must be a true comic
to forge these two together, to cleave
and cleave and fustian and fuss
over such scrutinizing eyes—one looking out
at a shadow people; the other,
making herself a shadow-puppet
to be played by no hand
but his.

Now, I pluck my eyebrows,
albeit carefully, keeping them "natural"
looking. Of course I'm a rebel:
I've got curly hair, don't I?

I remember, once, Papa in the yard, looking
past the broken fence, assessing damage
and seeing
an eye
thrust into a glass—the neighbor
in her bedroom, window flung high,
looking at herself in her vanity
and applying eyeliner or mascara
or some monstrosity that adds more legs and wisps
to life than a spider.

I don't recall who blinked more,
who looked away first. I remember the story afterward:
a cautionary tale of men who don't marry
the women they knew, but their mannequins,
trussed and forged with cosmetics.

Even now, there's a haunting
grip on my senses, that of another man.
He asks me to run to the woods

and the first thing I think is
but what will happen to my eyebrows?

All my years, avoiding mirrors, and
now—
this?

Papa was right to call me *vaidosa*—
always, he saw truth,
saw right through,
sawed through,
even 15 years and 3000 miles away.

Isn't that the way with everything?

Long after a hair is plucked,
I still sense the phantom tug
of its unearthing, its removal.
I am blind everywhere but
in the eyes. And now,
to him, I am incognito
everywhere,
but my voice.

If You Take the Light that Falls

for my Father

If you take the light that falls
between the firm hand at the end
of an extended arm that likes to trace
its fingers over cracks in the speckled wall
just outside of the old vineyard tucked
in lower Moitas-Venda, Portugal,

which we call "Moitas Baixa," as if it was
less an underworld—of which it seems, in its overhanging
of thickets, and relentless thorny lizards—and more a "downtown"
(those pink-painted houses—Old World versions
of turreted American Victorian homes—fool no one),
you can touch the ripeness of what isn't there; then, add

to it the senses inhaled and exhaled
while walking beside the mill inside Torres-Novas,
where the waterwheel, only half-rusted, is a fixed
point in time, and ducks cram for crusts
that never sog or sink, and utter their cacophonic
sighs of happiness and belonging without Portuguese accent. Now,

you begin to understand that these things
have an accumulation that is snug and tight.
But a comfortable snug and tight like a childhood
that was never yours, but your father's, a fantasy of orange
juices spilling from chin to ground in the valley
floor because there was always enough, but there isn't;

if you do all these things, and know all these things
are so often tasted strongest in memory, touched
most with blind fingers, felt hardest with solitude
ebbing in a quaint unnamed dingy shoring
up the Tagus River, you aren't going to be shocked by what
I have to tell you:

that is the scope, sum, weight, and size;
that is the heart, heat, and heft;
that is the earthy smell and rustic feel
of my love for you, big and baled up
as hay in the loitering *field* that has
a name in Portuguese, *campo,* that sounds like war.

But that's just fine, because I would wage and campaign and fight
any demon for you, or scale the walls of that place
where you stretch out, in your sleep, your long, malingering
fingers that disobey shadows, find all the cracks,
feel all the light with gluttony,
and take in the warmth that cools to your touch.

The Drowning Book

*for the 20-year-old woman in Dubai left to drown by her father, in
order to preserve her honor, 2015*

To separate a girl from water, call her "woman."
Let the word float like oil—albeit brief, as man's love,
his shout another silence, a cutting prow to part her like pages,
leave her rippling as a deckled edge. To die young,
a copy of Keats steeping in a pocket, is an impossible thing, reserved
for men like Shelley. Now we know not all mouths are meant for kissing
or keeping truths, like those of oceans and pitchers,
vessels that hold and convey water simultaneous
in their possessing and giving. Some mouths are meant for forging
holy echoes, round lips like stones, coins for the eyes.

To separate a life from living, call it "honor" and watch it sink
despite all claims, know better than to praise Ophelia and spare a Polonius
who passes for a father, letting her dissolve like a host on a tongue struggling
with prayer. Don't you see that water washes clean all things but words?
Even Keats worried of disuse and dispersal, diluted to a name writ on water.
But I'll freeze it for you—promise, for I am half-sick of shatters,
how the ledge of delusion is really a wave, a drawing of failing lips and
     curving hands
not finding a hold, instead a point, puncturing air with fingers that could be
     stroking.
They say woman was first a rib, curving half of punctuation, open
     parentheses, no closure—
a fissure in stone, a sliver in the ice. I say she is the Grail, sent to be refilled,
     too good for drinking.

Transformation

Revealing that nothing surrounds the heart more than mackerel,
the man sat down with his briny scent,
placed his fishmonger's hand on the bench's worn wood,
and cried his salted tears.

There is nothing as transformative
as a dream in which a man goes to sleep a man
and awakens a woman.

Between the Scantlings

from a line from Edgar Allan Poe's "The Tell-Tale Heart"

They've coveted whispers like cobwebs: stale
fragments of a life that sucked dry
the lives of others. Where there is venom

there is the refuse
and refusal of those who came before.
What warms this heart

can be anything hotter than an ice-cube:
with so little ways to go,
who can fail?

—

When they washed the windows, finally,
they found something unsought: light
that filtered between the beams, fustian
of rancid and remarkable
fusions of fanciful color,

a handicraft of the heavens! she exclaimed,
stopping in her tracks
with one hip pointing North
and a teacup quivering
beneath faded lips.

Don't be preposterous, said he of all the rage
without looking, who shook the rafters, cramped the crevices,
as if this house was a ship—sinking—
and he had to stop it up. *Don't fool yourself,*
she whispered. *It is.*

Reappearances

Who knows where disappearances are filed
in some hazy drawer,
where hope is the thing with claws
gouging out the eyes it mistakes for perches,
scattering the leaves.

When the easing became easier,
I sat with my chin pulled to my knees
(not the other way around)
as if I could eat myself, the legs
I hated in their short stumpiness.

This is the only way to make things work,
this doing yourself
and doing to yourself,
as my parents taught.
I could not see the rightness of ways

unless the sun was netted behind the trees
but now those trees are gone,
blasted from the earth by men my mother hired
to avoid a lawsuit, in case, one day,
that long-looked-for storm outside the house

would sweep those bent maples
in some hurricaning tumble
right over the stockade fence
and into the neighbor's yard.
"What if someone got killed?"

she asked before, with the same boredom
of a Modern woman drawing smoke
through her lungs, even though I know
my mother had never touched
a cigarette, had let one

touch her. This was her way of devouring
her senses before anyone would notice.
But the grace of her jawline
has been hidden for years,
the sadness of her eyes draped

upon every broken thing, mirroring
them. Is this the woman I know
looks nothing like me, yet holds
everything I believe in her heart
just the same? When I visit

the old house, I run to the yard
and worship the ground where roots
still push in lumps, still cry
to be seen and to trip and to
fall like the remains of a stacked wall,

of the fractured spine that doesn't know
the difference between being and breaking.
Do trees feel their phantom limbs? I want to know,
but there is no one to ask. I believe in trees
and ghosts, but have never considered the two

together, until now. Leaning over the roots,
I breathe so deep, it hurts my ribs.
I kick the ground not in anger but in pleasure,
my mouth and all its sighs of swallowing dirt,
the seizure of dust clouds: my repossession.

Where are all those things I once knew
would always be there, like the way
those three queer sisters cluttered
the yard, hanging broken talons
over the house-top. I was always

the one to give in to the clutches
just so I could push away the hands
and show them who was boss.
My parents never told me otherwise,
always said I could not do things

"because you are a girl,
that's why." So because I could not
do things, I did others, to compensate
and get around, to push beyond and
break the molds. No one would see

what hit them, I thought. No one
would know who I was all this time,
playing my games and waiting,
a little misshapen in some ways,
but not enough for anyone

to notice. There are some days
where I linger like a drifting leaf
snapped from its tether, and force
myself to float even long before
energy has run out. I think

I'll fall on someone's doorstep
and when they walk on me, I will shock them
with my crunch. I will make them wonder
*how did a leaf get here, in the dead
of winter? How bright—this unexpected thing.*

Aftermath

My father's asthma the catalyst,
I learned the meaning of "attack"
at the age of believing in flight with fingers
as pinions; how unbreakable were feathers,
too soft to wound. A word
both noun and verb, I marveled;
anything could be twice its appearance,
people—both beings and doings,

some questionably small things launched
into all the foreign places where no one feels them
until they hurt. After "attack,"
I learned the meaning of "hate,"
how connotation is the danger denotation
has to study with one eye
open; the other, a revolving door
of speculation and prayer.

A child, I thought "massacre" was acres
of Sunday services held beneath trees, brown
dots of devout faces, folded hands
tucked beneath chins like sliding messages
into envelopes, but never mailing them. Papa hung
a horseshoe over the family room door, *for good luck.*
All I saw was a crooked mouth, coming from the side,
an urgent cry, a massive jaw threatening

to clamp down on my bones, frail as an Ortolan's.
This will keep the evil out. Say a prayer to scare spirits—words
whistled from asthmatic lungs, soothing
as a kettle and its hot promise. I held up cupped hands.
"No, Papa," I wanted to say; "no. Not out.
It's keeping them in." How was I to know
that room was everything I would ever know,
a book of words hanging in air heavy with the steam of aftermath?

Appendix

after a photograph by Howard R. Debs, "Ice House, Rose Hill Manor"

They say God made man from clay but I know it was a block of ice,
    chiseled through.
Why else would earth last but not flesh?

When He gathered the seas, they were ice, and He could raise them all
    like nothing,
no need for spoons or saucers, prayer bowls or cupping hands.

How often we are deceived—that a singing bowl is actually a bell,
that a tree in a garden can be a ladder made from that tree,

rungs of knowledge and rails of life,
and no one around to climb it.

The river watering the garden separated in fourths, a part
snaking through Havilah where there is gold, some musty ancients say

—it is only chaff sunnying a poor patch of land,
a balding man scraping together a few coarse hairs to replenish his body

with the semblance of what would be humanity,
hungry and aching with thirst.

Why else the stones for ringing the mouth
of some mysterious lair, piled higher than cairns, cromlechs

collapsing upon themselves, unless God was disappointed,
as is told, in what we had become? See the under-lighting

nudging itself from the corner, the embers stoking out of sight.
Forget rest—the seventh day was for preparations kept secret.

To keep fingers to the outskirts is the simplest way, an act of levitation.
No man, just hands on a ledge, and the suspense is killing.

I'm not sure what we thought of Hell, or who was the first to envision it—
if we are meant to blame Eve, who has grown hobbled with the weight of
    scapegoating—

who birthed the first killer. But here hangs a cryptic knot
and pulley, as if this is a ship and its crew is disappointed

because the haul is no whale, no draught of 153 fish,
but a floating chunk of iceberg; that the sea is really straw

shimmied from a tidy windrow,
that the bulwark rising around it is not live oak but ragged-edged stones.

Recognize how purpose lends names—how "noose" and "knot" are two
    words
for the same thing. How one is made for a neck and another—anything else.

How there was traction and transom and transaction and all made-do with
    a simple lashing
together; now, there is taking and tying and trembling. O'Neill was right:

God is the iceman and He cometh; the covenant a distracting ruse,
and the flood of Noah's time reduced to a final, frozen cube—milky white

like an eye squaring us up, even still, polluted. *God sees all,*
even through this cataract. Our God

is a right hand, a *manus dei* in ancient texts and artwork,
clutching manacle, pinching force.

Consider this: there was no Serpent there until we came along and then—
it was too easy to say *yes.*

Who will do the lifting? Who to do the forcing forward
(or is it forging back)? Without passage of time,

there is no way to count movement
and up and down are fused, to push and pull,

to left and right, to right and wrong.
A body just out of sight but there enough to know how it foreshadows

man becoming insignificant, inconsequential. Unnecessary. A body
that evaporates like a pool, his reflection gone with it. What happens

when man himself is a vestigial organ? Worthless in a body,
worthwhile in a book, although even without it,

body and book exist. Here, take what's supplementary
and learn to make do. Turn your hands into a spade: work.

This is it, the final act, whether lifting or lowering. Everything comes down
to this: how we read ourselves from inside out.

Here are tongs like pulling a tooth, reminders of how we are all extractions,
how we are all so cold, how we need breaking

not molding or caressing; how hard we were once, like stone,
but never as lasting or strong.

Consider this: God as cruelest trickster; that ice is mistaken for a marble
    block
as easily as a marble block mistaken for ice,

and one will cool our fevers and the other break our teeth.
Know how all the bodies in a Roman museum can feel smoother than our
    own

and tempt us to wonder about sparseness, how Adam and Eve had aprons
of fig leaves but we—and Noah's dove—are given one leaf,

and forced to think it will suffice in keeping minds from straying.
He watches all, they repeat, unsure if they mean God or Christ

or Santa Claus, and maybe that's the Trinity, or there is someone else,
the understudy has stepped in, and this is the final curtain

call, or another rising—an encore and we are a desired performance,
	spontaneous dance
and we can choose to climb up or down. Maybe this is the matinee

and Lazarus has arrived on time, the director is already up to watch His
	work,
fingers on railing, ready to flee into a city of brick, not stone,

just out of frame, ready to hear the noise and muffle—ready to grow lost.
Us, so busy, unrecognizable and failing, turning trees into furniture.

All this time, we thought God was putting us in the world—
really, He was pulling us out.

Cristina J. Baptista is a first-generation Portuguese-American writer and educator whose work has appeared in *New Millennium Writings, Adanna, DASH, The Cortland Review, Structo, Right Hand Pointing*, and elsewhere. Her poem "Trouble Woman" was nominated by *Structo* in the 2016 Forward Prizes for Poetry. In 2012, a collection of her poetry won an Academy of American Poets Prize; in 2008, she won *The Baltimore Review's* Poetry Prize. She is also a 38th Voyager— one of 85 people in the world selected to travel on the 38th Voyage of the *Charles W. Morgan*, an 1841 wooden whaleship that is the last remaining one in the world. In collaboration with Mystic Seaport: The Museum of America and the Sea, Cristina wrote *Taking Her Back: Portuguese Presence & the 38th Voyage of the* Charles W. Morgan, a collection of poetry written while serving as one of the Voyagers. The collection documents the Portuguese immigrant experience aboard whaleships from the past through the present. Additionally, Cristina holds a Ph.D. in English from Fordham University in New York City. A scholar of Modern American Literature, she has presented her research on the Portuguese-American experience and Lusophonic presence in American literary works. Currently, Cristina teaches at a private school in Connecticut, where she also mentors an award-winning student-run literature and arts magazine and helps coordinate an annual Writers Festival for local high school students.

CPSIA information can be obtained
at www.ICGtesting.com
Printed in the USA
FFOW02n0558050317
33020FF